CW00594571

★ ★ ★ ★ ★ ★ ★ ★ ★ ★ ★

YOU MAY BE

50

But You've Still

GOT IT

★ ★ ★ ★ ★ ★ ★ ★ ★ ★ ★

summersdale

YOU MAY BE 50 BUT YOU'VE STILL GOT IT

Summersdale Publishers Ltd
46 West Street
Chichester
West Sussex
PO19 1RP
UK

www.summersdale.com

Printed and bound in China

ISBN: 978-1-84953-348-5

Substantial discounts on bulk quantities of Summersdale books are available to corporations, professional associations and other organisations. For details contact Nicky Douglas by telephone: +44 (0) 1243 756902, fax: +44 (0) 1243 756902 or email: nicky@summersdale.com.

To...... Tracy ....

From...... Edinburgh! ....

* * * * * * * * * * * *

LIFE IS EITHER A DARING ADVENTURE OR NOTHING.

HELEN KELLER

* * * * * * * * * * * *

★ ★ ★ ★ ★ ★ ★ ★ ★ ★ ★ ★ ★ ★

Now you're 50,
stop worrying about
what other people
think of *you!*

★ ★ ★ ★ ★ ★ ★ ★ ★ ★ ★ ★ ★ ★

* * * * * * * * * * *

Think about what you
wanted to be or do when
you grew up when
you were a child. Have
you achieved this?
It's not too late!

* * * * * * * * * * *

✦ ✦ ✦ ✦ ✦ ✦ ✦ ✦ ✦ ✦ ✦ ✦ ✦

If your family doesn't get together very often, host a *family barbecue* or dinner so everyone can *catch up.*

✦ ✦ ✦ ✦ ✦ ✦ ✦ ✦ ✦ ✦ ✦ ✦ ✦

★ ★ ★ ★ ★ ★ ★ ★ ★ ★ ★ ★ ★

Perform at an *open mic*
night and embrace your
inner superstar.

★ ★ ★ ★ ★ ★ ★ ★ ★ ★ ★ ★ ★

WHO KNOWS WHAT TOMORROW MAY BRING?

✦ ✦ ✦ ✦ ✦ ✦ ✦ ✦ ✦ ✦ ✦

Treat yourself to
a *massage* to ease
away the *strains* of
the working week.

✦ ✦ ✦ ✦ ✦ ✦ ✦ ✦ ✦ ✦ ✦

★ ★ ★ ★ ★ ★ ★ ★ ★ ★ ★ ★

On a pleasant day,
take a hike to your
county's highest point. Take
the opportunity as you're
walking to appreciate
the fresh air and
glorious views.

★ ★ ★ ★ ★ ★ ★ ★ ★ ★ ★ ★

★ ★ ★ ★ ★ ★ ★ ★ ★ ★ ★ ★

Buy a *pair of shoes*
or item of clothing that
you would normally pass
by because it is too
outrageous, and wear it
with pride.

★ ★ ★ ★ ★ ★ ★ ★ ★ ★ ★ ★

★ ★ ★ ★ ★ ★ ★ ★ ★ ★ ★

ANYTHING CAN BE
ACHIEVED.

★ ★ ★ ★ ★ ★ ★ ★ ★ ★ ★

* * * * * * * * * * * *

Smile at the person
who sits opposite you on
the train – maybe you
could even spark up a
conversation.

* * * * * * * * * * * *

★ ★ ★ ★ ★ ★ ★ ★ ★ ★ ★ ★

If your bedroom is
cluttered and untidy,
clear some space,
transforming it into a
pleasant and soothing
place to *relax.*

★ ★ ★ ★ ★ ★ ★ ★ ★ ★ ★ ★

★ ★ ★ ★ ★ ★ ★ ★ ★ ★ ★ ★

Research your
family history and
see what skeletons you can
dig up (metaphorically,
of course).

★ ★ ★ ★ ★ ★ ★ ★ ★ ★ ★ ★

Try making
sourdough bread:

★ To create a culture, mix 75 g each of flour and water, cover and leave somewhere warm to ferment.

★ Every 24 hours, add equal parts flour and water to 'feed' your yeast colony.

★ After a couple of days, the culture should be ready. Add 500 g more flour, 200 ml warm water and a pinch of salt and knead the mixture well until it forms the consistency of dough.

★ Leave to rise for around 10 hours, then bake it in a hot oven for 30 minutes. Voila!

★ ★ ★ ★ ★ ★ ★ ★ ★ ★ ★

BE THE PERSON
YOU WANT
TO BE.

★ ★ ★ ★ ★ ★ ★ ★ ★ ★

★ ★ ★ ★ ★ ★ ★ ★ ★ ★ ★ ★

Spread joy by giving people you meet a ***compliment*** about their appearance, mood, ideas... anything!

★ ★ ★ ★ ★ ★ ★ ★ ★ ★ ★ ★

* * * * * * * * * * * * *

Have your *portrait*
painted by an artist (or a
friend with artistic leanings)
and *put it up* in your home.

* * * * * * * * * * * * *

✱ ✱ ✱ ✱ ✱ ✱ ✱ ✱ ✱ ✱ ✱ ✱

Take a journey on the water; it could be anything from a luxurious cruise to navigating canals by *narrowboat.*

✱ ✱ ✱ ✱ ✱ ✱ ✱ ✱ ✱ ✱ ✱ ✱

✦ ✦ ✦ ✦ ✦ ✦ ✦ ✦ ✦ ✦ ✦ ✦

Learn basic *useful phrases* in several foreign languages. You never know when they might *come in handy!*

✦ ✦ ✦ ✦ ✦ ✦ ✦ ✦ ✦ ✦ ✦

★ ★ ★ ★ ★ ★ ★ ★ ★ ★ ★ ★

HAPPINESS DEPENDS UPON OURSELVES.

Aristotle

★ ★ ★ ★ ★ ★ ★ ★ ★ ★ ★ ★

✶ ✶ ✶ ✶ ✶ ✶ ✶ ✶ ✶ ✶ ✶ ✶

Get back to nature by
going camping and
taking the bare minimum
with you. Just remember to
tell someone where you're
going and avoid any
Bear Grylls heroics!

✶ ✶ ✶ ✶ ✶ ✶ ✶ ✶ ✶ ✶ ✶ ✶

* * * * * * * * * * * * *

Set yourself concrete *goals*
for the weeks, months and
years ahead, and ensure
you *achieve* them.

* * * * * * * * * * * * *

* * * * * * * * * * * *

Take some time to really get
to know the *children* in
your extended family, and
enjoy the wonderful and
funny things they
say and do.

* * * * * * * * * * * *

★ ★ ★ ★ ★ ★ ★ ★ ★ ★ ★ ★

Just because you're 50,
that doesn't mean you have
to stop *having fun!* For
your next birthday, hire a
bouncy castle!

★ ★ ★ ★ ★ ★ ★ ★ ★ ★ ★ ★

★ ★ ★ ★ ★ ★ ★ ★ ★ ★ ★

YOU *CAN* TEACH
OLD DOGS
NEW TRICKS.

★ ★ ★ ★ ★ ★ ★ ★ ★ ★ ★

★ ★ ★ ★ ★ ★ ★ ★ ★ ★ ★ ★

Even if you don't aspire
to be Jenson Button, book
a *track day* and tear
up the tarmac driving
a flash *sports car.*

★ ★ ★ ★ ★ ★ ★ ★ ★ ★ ★ ★

★ ★ ★ ★ ★ ★ ★ ★ ★ ★ ★ ★ ★

If you don't already, start *growing your own* produce. It could be anything from herbs in a window box to a grand *vegetable garden.*

★ ★ ★ ★ ★ ★ ★ ★ ★ ★ ★ ★ ★

★ ★ ★ ★ ★ ★ ★ ★ ★ ★ ★ ★

Go through your wardrobe
and donate everything that
you don't wear anymore
to a *charity shop.*
While you're there do some
shopping to replenish
your own wardrobe.

★ ★ ★ ★ ★ ★ ★ ★ ★ ★ ★ ★

* * * * * * * * * * * *

Audition to be an *extra*
in a film or television show.

* * * * * * * * * * * *

* * * * * * * * * *

WAKE UP
AND SMELL THE
COFFEE.

* * * * * * * * * * * *

* * * * * * * * * * * *

Learn about
aromatherapy, and
use it to help yourself
de-stress and *relax.*

* * * * * * * * * * * *

★ ★ ★ ★ ★ ★ ★ ★ ★ ★ ★ ★ ★

Take a week or two to go
on a *driving holiday*
around Europe. Have a
vague schedule, but be
flexible, allowing yourself
time to stay longer
in places that you
fall in love with.

★ ★ ★ ★ ★ ★ ★ ★ ★ ★ ★ ★ ★

★ ★ ★ ★ ★ ★ ★ ★ ★ ★ ★

Now you're
supposed to be one of
the more *'respectable'*
members of the family, why
not make a speech at a
family event? We'll start
you off: 'Unaccustomed as I
am to public speaking...'

★ ★ ★ ★ ★ ★ ★ ★ ★ ★ ★

★ ★ ★ ★ ★ ★ ★ ★ ★ ★ ★ ★

Learn to make your
favourite dish; the pride
of cooking it yourself will
make it twice as *delicious!*

★ ★ ★ ★ ★ ★ ★ ★ ★ ★ ★ ★

★ ★ ★ ★ ★ ★ ★ ★ ★ ★ ★

A SMILE
IS A GIFT THAT
CAN BE GIVEN
ENDLESSLY.

★ ★ ★ ★ ★ ★ ★ ★ ★ ★ ★

* * * * * * * * * * * *

Spend a long weekend
in the country — hire a
cabin or cottage for a few
nights, spending your days
exploring your surroundings
and your evenings curled up
in front of the fire, and see
if it makes you feel more
in touch with nature.

* * * * * * * * * * * *

★ ★ ★ ★ ★ ★ ★ ★ ★ ★ ★ ★

Visit the *circus* and
enjoy some old-fashioned
entertainment.

★ ★ ★ ★ ★ ★ ★ ★ ★ ★ ★ ★

* * * * * * * * * * * *

Think about each *decade*
of your life and what you
enjoyed most about them.
Combine all your best bits to
make sure your sixth decade
is the *best one yet.*

* * * * * * * * * * * *

* * * * * * * * * * *

A LIGHT HEART
LIVES LONG.

WILLIAM SHAKESPEARE

* * * * * * * * * * *

✶ ✶ ✶ ✶ ✶ ✶ ✶ ✶ ✶ ✶ ✶ ✶

Get on *a bus* without
checking the route and
see where it takes you —
you might end up finding a
new town or local beauty
spot you didn't know about!

✶ ✶ ✶ ✶ ✶ ✶ ✶ ✶ ✶ ✶ ✶ ✶

* * * * * * * * * * * *

Take the time to call
an *old friend* and
really *catch up* with them.

* * * * * * * * * * * *

★ ★ ★ ★ ★ ★ ★ ★ ★ ★ ★ ★

Brainstorm a list of things you'd really like to achieve or *improve* this year, and dedicate an hour a week to accomplishing them.

★ ★ ★ ★ ★ ★ ★ ★ ★ ★ ★ ★

★ ★ ★ ★ ★ ★ ★ ★ ★ ★ ★ ★

Really take the time to take
in and *appreciate* the
architecture of your
town or city.

★ ★ ★ ★ ★ ★ ★ ★ ★ ★ ★ ★

EVERY MOMENT
IS SPECIAL.

* * * * * * * * * * * *

Educate yourself
about a subject you think is
important but have never
had time to learn about.

* * * * * * * * * * * *

★ ★ ★ ★ ★ ★ ★ ★ ★ ★ ★ ★

Invest some of your
spending money in *shares;*
not enough to run any major
financial risks but enough
to *enjoy the thrill* of
playing the stock market.

★ ★ ★ ★ ★ ★ ★ ★ ★ ★ ★ ★

★ ★ ★ ★ ★ ★ ★ ★ ★ ★ ★ ★ ★

Learn to mix your favourite *cocktail*. Experiment with variations to make it *even better!*

★ ★ ★ ★ ★ ★ ★ ★ ★ ★ ★ ★ ★

★ ★ ★ ★ ★ ★ ★ ★ ★ ★ ★

YOU'RE ONLY EVER AS OLD AS YOU FEEL.

★ ★ ★ ★ ★ ★ ★ ★ ★ ★ ★

* * * * * * * * * * * *

Volunteer your time
reading to children —
reading aloud is not only
fantastic fun and a
bonding experience between
you and the children, but it
will allow you to really
focus on the words.

* * * * * * * * * * * *

✶ ✶ ✶ ✶ ✶ ✶ ✶ ✶ ✶ ✶ ✶ ✶

Try *backpacking* or youth
hostelling with a club or
through a holiday organiser.
It'll be an opportunity to
meet like-minded people
and make *new friends.*

✶ ✶ ✶ ✶ ✶ ✶ ✶ ✶ ✶ ✶ ✶ ✶

* * * * * * * * * * * * *

Throughout your life, which
books have you found the
most affecting or enjoyable?
Reread them and see
what you think now.

* * * * * * * * * * * * *

★ ★ ★ ★ ★ ★ ★ ★ ★ ★ ★ ★

Try to make *smiling* your
default facial *expression.*

★ ★ ★ ★ ★ ★ ★ ★ ★ ★ ★ ★

WHEN DESTINY CLOSES A DOOR, IT OPENS A WINDOW.

✦ ✦ ✦ ✦ ✦ ✦ ✦ ✦ ✦ ✦ ✦ ✦

Organise and shoot a
calendar to raise money
for a charity close to your
heart. No one is saying you
have to take your kit off, but
it's an option!

✦ ✦ ✦ ✦ ✦ ✦ ✦ ✦ ✦ ✦ ✦ ✦

* * * * * * * * * * * *

Research the history of
your home and your local
area; you may find something
that *surprises you.*

* * * * * * * * * * * *

* * * * * * * * * * *

Take your partner or a friend
ice skating in winter at an
outdoor rink, then warm up
afterwards with a steaming
glass of *mulled wine.*

* * * * * * * * * * *

* * * * * * * * * * *

Spend a day
documenting your life
on a camcorder or your
mobile phone. You could
do something special with
your day, or just record your
everyday activities – it
will still be an interesting
record of your personality
and lifestyle.

* * * * * * * * * * *

★ ★ ★ ★ ★ ★ ★ ★ ★ ★ ★ ★

TRY NEW THINGS.

★ ★ ★ ★ ★ ★ ★ ★ ★ ★ ★ ★

★ ★ ★ ★ ★ ★ ★ ★ ★ ★ ★ ★ ★

Visit a local residential
or *care home* and
spend some time talking or
playing games with
the residents.

★ ★ ★ ★ ★ ★ ★ ★ ★ ★ ★ ★ ★

* * * * * * * * * * * *

Spend a day with a
close friend and allow
them to make all the choices
about your activities. You'll
find out more about them,
yourself, and maybe get a
new hobby along the way.

* * * * * * * * * * * *

* * * * * * * * * * * *

Redecorate your home as creatively and as suited to your own tastes as you can. If you want that 6 ft giraffe statue, you can *have it!*

* * * * * * * * * * * *

* * * * * * * * * * *

Bake a cake and make it
your best ever, whether it's
your first or your *101st.*

* * * * * * * * * * *

* * * * * * * * * * * *

THERE IS MORE TO LIFE THAN INCREASING ITS SPEED.

MAHATMA GANDHI

* * * * * * * * * * * *

★ ★ ★ ★ ★ ★ ★ ★ ★ ★ ★ ★

Take a *holiday* to
somewhere with a history
that interests you. See if you
can learn *a few facts*
you didn't know.

★ ★ ★ ★ ★ ★ ★ ★ ★ ★ ★ ★

* * * * * * * * * * * *

Strike up a *conversation*
with someone on public
transport or in a waiting
room. Everyone has an
interesting story to tell.

* * * * * * * * * * * *

✦ ✦ ✦ ✦ ✦ ✦ ✦ ✦ ✦ ✦ ✦ ✦ ✦

Try your hand at a new *crafting* hobby – it can be as simple as melting beeswax and pouring into attractive tea cups to create your own candles, or as complex as creating a patchwork blanket *from scratch!*

✦ ✦ ✦ ✦ ✦ ✦ ✦ ✦ ✦ ✦ ✦ ✦ ✦

* * * * * * * * * * * *

Dig out your old
record collection and
play albums back to back,
to bring some nostalgia into
your life. If you no longer
own a record player, then
that's what *YouTube* is for!

* * * * * * * * * * * *

★ ★ ★ ★ ★ ★ ★ ★ ★ ★

IF LIFE GIVES YOU LEMONS, MAKE LEMONADE.

★ ★ ★ ★ ★ ★ ★ ★ ★ ★

* * * * * * * * * * * *

Get involved with your local *community* and help organise or run a *summer fete,* or volunteer at an animal shelter or charity shop.

* * * * * * * * * * * *

✶ ✶ ✶ ✶ ✶ ✶ ✶ ✶ ✶ ✶ ✶

Increase your *fitness*
level by pledging to get
off your bus a stop early or
take the stairs rather
than the lift.

✶ ✶ ✶ ✶ ✶ ✶ ✶ ✶ ✶ ✶ ✶

✦ ✦ ✦ ✦ ✦ ✦ ✦ ✦ ✦ ✦ ✦ ✦ ✦

Send an anonymous
gift to a friend or family
member you know is having
a hard time.

✦ ✦ ✦ ✦ ✦ ✦ ✦ ✦ ✦ ✦ ✦ ✦ ✦

* * * * * * * * * * *

Finally *master* the
Rubik's cube.

* * * * * * * * * * *

★ ★ ★ ★ ★ ★ ★ ★ ★ ★ ★

THE WORLD IS YOUR OYSTER.

★ ★ ★ ★ ★ ★ ★ ★ ★ ★ ★

* * * * * * * * * * * *

Take a moment
to think about how the
world has changed
since you were born. Think
of all the new *inventions*
that have made life easier,
safer and more fun in
the last fifty years.

* * * * * * * * * * * *

* * * * * * * * * * * * *

Watch a *foreign film*
without the subtitles turned
on to see how much of the
plot you can understand
by just the visuals and
the *emotion* in the
actors' voices.

* * * * * * * * * * * * *

* * * * * * * * * * * *

Write *haikus* (poems of
three lines, the first and third
line having five syllables, the
middle one having seven)
in letters and cards to your
loved ones.

* * * * * * * * * * * *

★ ★ ★ ★ ★ ★ ★ ★ ★ ★ ★

IT'S NEVER TOO LATE TO CHANGE YOUR LIFE.

★ ★ ★ ★ ★ ★ ★ ★ ★ ★ ★

★ ★ ★ ★ ★ ★ ★ ★ ★ ★ ★ ★

Use your *arts and crafts*
skills to make by hand the
next *gift* you intend to
give someone.

★ ★ ★ ★ ★ ★ ★ ★ ★ ★ ★ ★

★ ★ ★ ★ ★ ★ ★ ★ ★ ★ ★ ★ ★

Get a *pen friend* and
write to each other as
often as possible. Try to
write to someone from
another country so you can
experience their *culture.*

★ ★ ★ ★ ★ ★ ★ ★ ★ ★ ★ ★ ★

★ ★ ★ ★ ★ ★ ★ ★ ★ ★ ★ ★ ★

Hire a *glitzy car* for
the day, and see how many
people you can convince
that you have won
the *lottery.*

★ ★ ★ ★ ★ ★ ★ ★ ★ ★ ★ ★ ★

★ ★ ★ ★ ★ ★ ★ ★ ★ ★ ★ ★ ★

Invest in a *small hive,*
some protective gear and
equipment and learn how to
keep bees.

★ ★ ★ ★ ★ ★ ★ ★ ★ ★ ★ ★ ★

* * * * * * * * * * * *

Take a *day off work*
and spend it at home, in
your garden, enjoying the
quiet. Perhaps read a book,
or *cut some flowers*
for your home.

* * * * * * * * * * * *

★ ★ ★ ★ ★ ★ ★ ★ ★ ★ ★

REALISE THE IMPORTANCE OF YOU.

* * * * * * * * * * * *

When you're researching
holidays this year choose
somewhere you've never
considered before — swap
a luxury city break for an
adventure holiday in
Europe, or swap your beach
holiday for a weekend of
scouring the markets
of Marrakech.

* * * * * * * * * * * *

✦ ✦ ✦ ✦ ✦ ✦ ✦ ✦ ✦ ✦ ✦ ✦

Visit your *old school*
and see how much the
place has *changed.*

✦ ✦ ✦ ✦ ✦ ✦ ✦ ✦ ✦ ✦ ✦ ✦

✦ ✦ ✦ ✦ ✦ ✦ ✦ ✦ ✦ ✦ ✦ ✦

Apply for tickets to see
your *favourite TV show*
being filmed. It'll more than
likely be free, an evening
of *good fun* and a
new experience.

✦ ✦ ✦ ✦ ✦ ✦ ✦ ✦ ✦ ✦ ✦ ✦

NOTHING VENTURED, NOTHING GAINED.

★ ★ ★ ★ ★ ★ ★ ★ ★ ★ ★

Try making your
own beer or wine, using
a *home-brewing* or
winemaking kit.

★ ★ ★ ★ ★ ★ ★ ★ ★ ★ ★

* * * * * * * * * * *

Call an *elderly family*
member for a chat.
Ask them to relate their
fondest memory,
in as much detail as
they can.

* * * * * * * * * * *

＊ ＊ ＊ ＊ ＊ ＊ ＊ ＊ ＊ ＊ ＊

Look forward to what you
hope to *achieve* and
experience by your
sixtieth birthday.

＊ ＊ ＊ ＊ ＊ ＊ ＊ ＊ ＊ ＊ ＊

* * * * * * * * * * * * *

Write a letter to your
60-year-old self and keep it
somewhere safe for you to find
again in *ten years' time.*

* * * * * * * * * * * * *

* * * * * * * * * * * *

THE MOST IMPORTANT THING IS TO ENJOY YOUR LIFE - TO BE HAPPY - IT'S ALL THAT MATTERS.

AUDREY HEPBURN

* * * * * * * * * * * *

If you're interested in finding out more about our gift books, follow us on Twitter: @Summersdale

www.summersdale.com